30 Day Money Challenge

TAKE CONTROL OF YOUR FINANCES, ONE DAY AT A TIME

BY

ZINNIA ADAMS

Get Your Free Money Moves Starter Kit
Here-→ https://bit.ly/PStarterkit

Join My Private FB Community HERE
-→ www.facebook.com/groups/goaldiggerzrus

www.perspectiveschange.com

Table of Contents

Why I Wrote This Book

I am a single mother of at the point of this book a soon to be 18 year old. I am a working class woman with an interesting background. I was not always good with money. In fact, I was bad with it. I've been through a lot of financial woes which is why I can relate and chose to write this book. Raising a child by yourself can certainly have a strain on your finances. I have learned a lot of lessons through my failures and I'm not ashamed to admit them.

I come not to tell where you went wrong but help you figure out how to get right.

I grew up as the youngest of three to a teenage single mother. I learned quickly about life without money. This created a misconception that having money would solve ALL my problems. Eventually I learned life is not all about having money but about what you do with the money you have. Working hard to get a substantial salary will not solve your money problems, it might create some new ones for you if you are not careful.

One day I will write a book about the story of how I went from being a 17 year old single mother not even knowing what credit was, being evicted on the streets and filing bankruptcy to graduating with my Bachelor's degree debt free, traveling the world, and earning a 750 credit score.

I am proud of where I come from it helps me appreciate where I am and where I am headed. My old school working glass upbringing truly orders a lot of my steps presently. Life is a learning experience that never ends. Working class people come from all walks of life and truly make the world go round. This challenge is about understanding those differences and realizing that things happen, what matters is what we do next.

I created Perspectives to make a difference and truly inspire individuals to have more conversations about money. I want money to be an open discussion and one that we have more with our children.

Perspectives empowers individuals to take control of their finances and end the paycheck to paycheck cycle. Sometimes it is hard to get started but this challenge will get you fired up give you a whole new look on your finances.

Let's Make Personal Finance a Family Heirloom

Who Is This Book For?

T his book is not for you if you are not serious about your finances. If you are not ready to step out of your comfort zone and be honest about your current money situation, I would suggest you put the book down now. I am very passionate about personal finance and want to help and inspire others.

There are no income requirements. It is simply a tool. This book is in no way financial advice. It should also be noted that I am not a financial advisor and this information is strictly for informational purposes.

This book IS for you if you get paid on Friday and you are broke by Monday?

This book IS for you if you can budget like a boss when you're broke but on payday you just throw it in the cart.

This book IS for you if can't answer your phone because of debt collectors.

This book IS for you if you want to travel but can never find the funds.

This book IS for you if you are jealous of friends who living their best life and you have no idea how they can afford it.

Finally, this book IS for you if you are ready to change your relationship with money and finally reach financial goals. *30 Day Money Challenge*

30 Day Money Challenge

Create Spending Tracker	Check Reports	DeCode Paycheck	Create Budget	Acct Statements	Spending Test	Total Debt
Debt Repayment Plan	Review All Bills	Open A Savings Acct	Auto Savings	Emergency Fund??	Spending Test	Evaluate Triggers
Review Expense Tracker	Find Lunch Recipes	Side Hustle???	Expense	Method Begins	Spring Cleaning	Spending Test
CC's on Punishment	X Credit Card	2nd Expense	Set Savings Goals	Calculate Retirement	Determine Net Worth	Spending Test
Big Picture						

The Coins Cache

Use the calendar as a guide, we will discuss daily activities throughout the book.

Each day is designed to take a look at another aspect that might be delaying your financial success. Remember, do what's best for you. Follow the steps in a different order if you like, as long as you complete the challenge.

Join our Facebook Community The Goal Diggerz Community

PERSPECTIVES

Making Personal Finance a Family Heirloom

Get Prepared

When working on your money, it doesn't work to just jump in. Put in the time to prepare. When going on a diet there is usually time spent at the store buying the proper food. You have to check your wardrobe to make sure you have gym shoes and work out gear. Finances are no different.

Get Serious

One important factor in everything you do is that you have to be in it to win it. Reading this book by itself is not enough. Doing what you have always done is not working so it is time to make some changes. That's why I named my company Perspectives. Nothing will be done

5

until you make the necessary changes. TODAY is the day!!! Change your perspectives about money. Make the decision to get serious about your finances and your financial future… and then teach your children.

Be Honest

This 30 Day Money Challenge is a great tool and can give you the push you need to change your financial outlook. Get Prepared, Get Serious, and Be Honest with yourself. You will come away with realistic goals identified and knowledge of the necessary steps needed to achieve them. Being dishonest throughout the process will only hurt yourself. I wish you the best of luck and see you on the other side.

Lets discuss it in our Facebook Community The Goal Diggerz Community.

Look In the Mirror

Day 1

The first activity is to look in the mirror. Begin tracking expenses daily for 14 days. Track everything! If you buy an item that's 25 cents make sure you track it. Track any donation at work, money you give to the person in the middle of the street with a sign- Track *everything*. This first step is important because you will need to analyze your spending habits.

The Savvy Budget Planner is perfect for this activity. It comes with an expense tracker layout to help you get a grip on spending. If you are not honest with yourself during this step, it will affect the rest of the challenge. You will only be cheating yourself. Sometimes it can be hard to record all purchases as soon as they happen. Record it in the memo app on your phone and add it to your tracker later, if that works better for you.

Are You Checking??

Day 2

D id you know that you are entitled to a free copy of your credit report annually at www.annualcreditreport.com? Looking at what's on your credit report is the second step to seeing where you are at. Find out who you owe and how much. Start looking at the big picture of what you are dealing with. The point of this challenge is to get an idea of your entire financial situation, not just your savings or your budget.

There are three credit bureaus: Experian, Equifax, and Transunion. Information reported on your credit reports varies between the three bureaus. Different creditors report to different bureaus, so requesting just one is not enough. Simply go on the website and it will connect you with each bureau individually. Make sure you save copies of your file on your computer. If you plan to print, make sure you have plenty of ink and paper as the reports are quite lengthy in size. Here are some great pins about credit here.

Take this time to become familiar with your credit report and understand it. Once you are aware of how it works, you can act accordingly. Check about my blog post about being aware of what's on your credit here.

Where Is Your Money Going?

Day 3

---○---

Today let's review your paycheck and pay attention to the deductions. This process is all about finding out where your money is going and deciding where it should go. Continuing with the beginning theme of the week, we are taking an eye-opening look at what we are dealing with. The next step is to review your paycheck and decode it. When looking for employment we usually have standards, but rarely do we actually bring home that amount. For example, if I make $50,000 a year, after deductions I am not coming close to that amount.

This also might be a time to consider W4 elections. The amount of exemptions entered on your W4 determines how much taxes will be taken out of each paycheck. Please consider that when filling out forms upon hiring. If you need help and want to know more please visit Investopedia's website.

Tell Your Money What To Do

Day 4

───────○───────

Let's talk about that word that keeps everybody up at night. Budget is a nice word and one that will change your entire life. I think that many people make it scarier and more complicated than it has to be. A budget is a plan for your money. Don't begin this journey without giving your money a plan. There will be ups and downs. There will be impulse buys and days when you will fall completely off and that's ok!

The purpose of a budget is to determine the amount of money coming in (assets) and compare it with how much money is going out (liabilities) every month. This has many purposes: you can find out if you make enough money to cover your monthly expenses, determine just how much money you have available to pay off debt or put away for other things like travel and new car purchases, and you can also use a budget to determine if there is a need to pick up an additional income while working on reducing debt/creating disposable income.

List your income, develop a figure to reflect your incoming assets per month. If you have a variable income, such as commission or service based industry, the best way to determine income is to use an average based on a rolling three month period. Next, list your expenses.

Subtract your expenses from your income. This money can be used to pay off debt, additional savings, or other goals. Some choose to use the 50/30/20 rule and allocate 50% to debt repayment, 30% to additional savings, and 20% to investments. Notice I said <u>additional</u> savings, but we will get to that later. We discuss this in my Facebook Community The GOAL Diggerz Community.

Review Account Statements

Day 5

———————○———————

This one might be eye opening. Go online and review credit card and bank account statements for the previous 6 months. Most of the time when I tell others to pay themselves *FIRST*, their first rebuttal is that they don't have any money to save. While this may be true some of the time, it is absolutely not the truth most of the time. If you can review your statements for the past 6 months and not find 6 purchases that are not a necessity, then and only then I'll believe you don't have the ability to save.

The purpose of this exercise is to help you be more aware of where your money is going and decide if that's where it should be going.

While reviewing your statements, be sure to add up all the purchases that were not necessities. Even if you choose to round up, give yourself a total spent in those 6 months. Now think about other uses for that money savings, investing, travel… the options are endless

First Spending Test

Day 6

―――――――○―――――――

L et's challenge ourselves in this 30 Day Money Challenge. A spending test is a challenge of discipline. There are several spending tests through this challenge designed to help you gradually take control of spending. Think about your guilty pleasures. This is something that you purchase all the time like a cup of coffee, hair salon, snacks, etc. Pick something that you normally purchase regularly. If you are having trouble deciding on what to refrain from, use your expense tracker. Review your tracker and choose the item purchased the most that is not a necessity.

The first step to taking control of your finances is creating good financial habits. So take strides to get rid of the bad habits, one step at a time. We are now make the conscious decision to minimize purchases of this item. If we buy it every day I would limit it to 4 times a week. I built spending tests into my Money Challenge to help you become more disciplined gradually. If cold turkey works best for you, feel free to completely stop.

Face The Facts

Day 7

───────────○───────────

Today is an eye opening day. Do you know the total amount of debt that you owe? Beginning this journey was a bold step. I am proud that you made it this far and it is not time to turn back now. It's hard to really see the fight a head without knowing exactly what you are up against. You made a commitment that will change your life when you started this challenge.

Collect account balances. Use your credit reports, account statements, known bills, and mail. Just because it is not on your credit report doesn't mean it is not counted. Count every balance that you owe. Sometimes you might find it difficult to stay focused. This will help you put things into perspective. Knowing how much debt you owe has its own way of putting purchases in a different light. This exercise will help you realize why you need a budget.

If you have payday loans, title loans, even loans from your retirement accounts, all those number should be counted. If you're behind in your rent, add the amount that would bring it current. This is your golden number and knowing this figure that will help you become debt free.

What Are You Going To Do About It?

Day 8

So to recap, we have a few things understood at this point. We now are completely aware of where our money is going. We are already on a great path to building great spending habits by eliminating frivolous purchases. We identified the magic number that will take our net worth from a negative to a positive. The only thing to do at this point is to develop a <u>debt repayment plan</u>. What are our goals? What is it that you are planning to accomplish financially?

Are you starting to feel better about your financial situation? Not yet?... keep reading. Make a plan and estimate your debt free date. After doing your budget, you know how much disposable income is available every month. So you know how much money is available for debt repayment.

Put all your debt in perspective. I love using <u>Undebt.it</u> to plug in all of my balances. This website allows you to plug in all of your current balances, interest rates, and minimum payments. It is a great tool that allows you to view all your debt in one place. Pay attention to how much interest you are paying every month, because it might make you sick to your stomach. Interest can be your best friend or your worst enemy. Decide which debt to attack first. I would suggest the Snow Avalanche method which pays off debt based on the highest interest rate. You could also combine multiple methods whatever gets you there sooner. Undebt.it also gives you the projected date you will be debt free and it updates accordingly when extra payments are made.

Big Picture

Day 9

Let's shake things up. Ok, we got a budget and a debt repayment plan. Wouldn't it be great if you could create some extra money to help pay off debt quicker? Well the answer is not running and getting a 2nd job (just yet). Even if you reviewed your budget and decided that you did not make enough income, the first thing to do is correct bad habits before adding more money. More money will not fix your problems! You must first correct your financial faux pas.

The purpose of Day 9 is to review your bills and see where you can cut it. Do you need cable? Do you need the unlimited everything plan with your cell phone company? Review these bills and see if you are able to cut them. Start making sure the lights are turned off when leaving the room, and don't let the water run while you get ready to get in the shower. Wait until you are ready to get in and then turn the water on. These minor changes are great ways for you to find money in the current budget you already have. Minimize bills that you have now to create more disposable income.

This is also a good time to plot due dates on a calendar. I personally use <u>Prism</u> to help keep me on track with my bills. They are consistent about reminding you when you haven't paid. There is no obligation to pay through the app, I simply use the app for bill reminders.

Open A Savings Account

Day 10

To help push along your savings or if you are someone who finds it hard to put money away from savings, I usually suggest they get a separate savings account. It is simply to build savings. Do your research on high interest savings accounts. One of my favorite options is the Digital Credit Union.

If you already have multiple savings accounts, then simply identify the least accessible and get rid of any debit card or online access that you have. This account is strictly for incoming funds no withdrawals allowed. Make this commitment for yourself.

Like Clock Work

Day 11

Now that the account is set up and dedicated to savings ONLY, you will need to set up automatic savings deposits. Set it and Forget is the name of the game. Automatic withdrawals or transfers into your savings will help you automate your savings and put you first. After time it will surprise you how you learn to operate without those funds. Go to your employer and adjust your direct deposit information. Set a percentage of your income or a set amount to be deposited directly into the designated savings account you isolated yesterday and then forget about it. Paying yourself first is the name of the game.

I preach Pay Yourself First because if you don't, there will be nothing to come behind you and force you to put away those savings. If you don't pay your bills they have great ways of motivating you to provide payment, but who is there to make sure you take care of you?

Emergency Fund??

Day 12

───────────○───────────

Do you have an <u>emergency fund</u>? If your car broke down today, are you able to pay for repairs without disrupting current obligations? This is an important question that unfortunately the average individual's answer will be no. This is a problem. Even when you are working to pay down debt, it is important to have an emergency fund and it will help you stay on track should an unexpected expense arise. Having to use your credit card because you didn't have any savings will delay your journey to debt freedom. So don't wait... Start today!!!

How much should an emergency fund be? This is debatable. I would suggest at least 3-5 months of your full monthly overhead costs. This will definitely ease your mind should an emergency arise and prevent you from falling off track so easily. It also gives you a different kind of peace of mind. You are not as stressed when you know you have money to cover the unexpected emergency.

Second Spending Test

Day 13

F or this test, there are two options: you can further limit the expense from the first spending test. For example: if you dropped from buying coffee from 7 days a week to 4 days a week, at this point drop it down to 2 days a week. Depending on how much sugar and cream you add to your coffee, your waistline might thank you along with your wallet. Choose an item that you THINK is a necessity. It doesn't have to be a specific item- it can be a store.

Self Reflection

Day 14

Today let's think about why we spend. Are you an emotional spender? Is it a hobby or your favorite pastime? Some people love the excitement of purchasing things. They call it retail therapy. Whatever your trigger is, if you reflect and start to pay attention and keep an open mind, you might develop the reason for some of your spending. Is it just out of habit that you walk past this establishment every day and you always buy something?

The reason you should evaluate your triggers is because we don't want to only identify our shortcomings, we want to work towards resolving them to help reach our financial goals. This *is* the 30 Day Money Challenge, after all. Challenge spending.

What Did The Mirror Say?

Day 15

After two weeks of tracking all of our spending, today is an eye opening moment when we look back and what we spent our money on. Look for recurring charges, look for restaurant charges.

Look for convenience stores and department stores. Some of the purchases might be necessities but only minimally. If we are on the path to debt freedom, it's important that first we are honest with ourselves and secondly, we are not in denial. The important part about this challenge is learning more about our relationship with finances and changing our perspectives.

Don't like what you see? Let's decide what we are going to do about it.

Look On Lunch

Day 16

What does lunch at work look like for you? Mine looks very similar to lunch at home. Set a goal to start prepping your lunches for the work week. This will help save tons of money. Look at the expense tracker and see how much money was spent on restaurants. Let's drop that number down.

If prepping is an issue, consider crockpot recipes or head over to Google for some quick homemade lunch ideas. This money can now be set for debt repayment and savings. One of my favorite cooking sites is Allrecipes.

Side Hustle Much???

Day 17

Now that a budget has been created, we have evaluated our debt, made some cuts and started to work on our discipline. Based on our debt repayment plan, we've determined how long it will take before we are debt free.

If you use Undebt.it this will be the number in the top right hand corner. If this number doesn't please you or you still have issues creating disposable income to pay off debt, maybe consider getting a side hustle. This can be in the form of an additional job or using a skill you already have. Have you ever thought about becoming a public speaker? Check out my blog post for other ideas.

Think about different ways to make extra money. All of it can go towards debt as additional payments you might want to decide on a percentage maybe 50/50. 50% towards debt and 50% savings.

You Need To Cut It

Day 18

———————o———————

E valuate your monthly expenses. Is there anything that can afford to be cut (even if it's temporary) to help you reach your financial goals faster? I made the decision to cut cable in 2012 when I decided I wanted to get my bachelor's degree without any student loans. It was hard because I felt like I needed it to see my TV shows. The truth of the matter is that once in school full time and working full time, I never had any real time to watch those TV shows anymore anyway.

Here I am 7 years later and I still have not returned to cable. This was one of the best decisions I ever made for my wallet. In case you are wondering, I did in fact graduate debt free with no loans as a single parent. Some things might be easier to cut like downgrading to basic service as opposed to premium services.

Try Something New

Day 19

―――――○―――――

Have you ever heard of the envelope method? Sometimes regular budgeting tips don't work for individuals. I always make it my business to provide some alternate options. The goal in this journey is to find out what works for YOU. Some individuals might like to try other methods. The envelope method is a cash budget system. Each envelope is labeled with the expense that it represents. When creating a budget for the following month, list all the expenses in their own individual envelope.

When you get paid, be sure to withdraw the cash needed for your budgeted expenditures. Make sure luxuries as well as necessities are accounted for. The reason for this is once your cash is gone, your cash is gone. There is no moving cash amongst envelopes and once you have spent all the money for a particular item, you are not to touch any additional funds unless it's an emergency.

The purpose of the exercise is to help you be more mindful when you are exceeding your budget. It is very easy to continue swiping when transactions are not updated in real time and it can also make it hard to keep up with your balance. Most people get paid on Friday, so by the time Monday comes after paying bills and other impulse buys, they are unaware of how much money they really have until their accounts update on Monday morning. It is usually at this point they realize they are broke for the next two weeks.

Spring Cleaning

Day 20

This is a fun day for me. On this day, set aside and go through your closets and other storage. If it hasn't been used in the last 6 months (or even better- a year), get rid of it. Sell it or donate it if it's in good condition. Sometimes you have to let go of the old. After all, we are working on our best financial life.

Same rule applies to that wallet. If you haven't been to the gym in 6 months, why are you still paying for that membership? When you are ready to get physically fit, YouTube is a great way to start for free until you graduate to the gym. Take into account subscription services and other memberships too. If they are not being used, cut them. The money that you used to use for these items has a debt with its name on it now.

If you need to, feel free to rearrange this day until your off day and do another the task from another day in its place.

Third Spending Test

Day 21

The Third Spending Test is a way to step even further out of your comfort zone. Let's not forget the purpose of this test is to focus on being fiscally disciplined. At this point you should have gotten into a rhythm with the expenses used for previous spending tests. You will simply use this day to focus on limiting the purchase of an additional item, store, or service. This might be a daily trip to a fast food restaurant or even convenience store. Limit this purchase or eliminate and item that you previously minimized.

Take into account subscription services and other memberships too. If they are not being used, cut them. The money that you used to use for these items has a debt with its name on it now.

Credit Cards on Punishment

Day 22

On Day 22, I want you to remove all credit cards from your wallet. Out of sight, out of mind. Put them in your unmentionables drawer or even give them to a trusted family member or friend. It's hard to pay off debt while still creating it. Having your credit cards easily accessible makes it that much easier to swipe them. You don't feel the pressure until that bill comes at the end of the month.

When working to pay off debt, it can be like taking two steps back if still using credit cards. This will not only slow down your financial journey but limit funds if a real emergency arises.

Those who build up miles- trust me- I hear you and I understand. Don't get mad at me. However this is a temporary sacrifice to build discipline and craft your financial future.

Delete Credit Cards

Day 23

Now on day 23, delete your credit card info from all online platforms. Delete credit cards from all accounts. If you don't have the cash for the purchase that means you don't need it.

Temptation is a beast… so during this journey it might be best to delete shopping apps that you normally use as well. Also delete all those sale emails you get which inspire you to make impulse purchases. Impulse shopping is one of the number one budget killers. You don't have to go through them all at once- just simply unsubscribe as you see them.

Cut Second Expense

Day 24

Do you use any of the recent new service? I focus on them because not too long ago we all lived without them and life was alright. Day 24 is all about cutting another expense. This is simply to minimize monthly overhead to create more disposable income. Might be a temporary fix might be a long term- that's something for you to decide. In the meantime you need to cut it.

Set Goals

Day 25

Determine your long term and short term savings goals. Will you need a car in the near future? Need a down payment for a house? It's important to have a savings account for household repairs or for emergencies.

Short term savings goals are important also. Have a dream trip you want to go on? Saving regularly towards the trip will feel much better to your wallet than lump sum payments.

Take the time to write down what these goals are and how much is needed for each goal…. puts things into perspective.

Payday When You're Old & Grey

Day 26

How much thought have you given to retirement? Don't wait till you're old and grey to put some pennies away today. The best tool one could possibly use to save for retirement is TIME.

Saving for retirement can seem daunting and overwhelming. Where do you start? Try this retirement income calculator on Vanguard's website. How much do you need? I won't get into detail but the task today is to ask yourself some important questions.

How much money do I need to make in retirement? Will I be renting? Owning? Assisted living?

How much do I currently have saved for retirement?

How much do I need?

Does my company provide a match? If so how much? What are the terms? Am I vested?

What's Really In Your Wallet?

Day 27

---o---

D o you know your net worth? Your net worth is calculated by subtracting your liabilities from your assets. This goal in this challenge is to increase this number by eliminating debt and creating better financial habits.

An asset is something that brings in money and a liability is something that takes away money. That to me is the clearest definition possible. It doesn't get much simpler than that.

Fourth Spending Test

Day 28

A t this point you know the drill. Hey Hey Hey, what are we cutting today? Make the decision to minimize an expense you have already limited. Or choose something new to cut. Do you run late all the time and find yourself using a rideshare service every day? Why?

Leave out early and save your coins.

SWOT

Day 29

---○---

We've had some eye opening moments and revelations. There might have been some that disappointed you and that's ok. In this exercise you will perform a SWOT analysis on yourself. Strengths, Weaknesses, Opportunities and Threats of your financial journey. That's why we're here. That was the whole point- to get a clear idea of your strengths and weaknesses in regard to your financial situation. What is a threat to your journey and what will be opportunities for you to improve your current financial habits?

Spread The Word

Day 30

N ow spread the word. Let your friends and family know about your goals. Taking on this journey will not be easy. It's important they know that you missing some events is not lack of support on your end, but an increase in financial responsibility. Penny pinching is not a way of life, but sometimes it's necessary to get where we need to be.

Don't forget to join my Facebook Group The GOAL DIggerz Community

www.ingramcontent.com/pod-product-compliance
Lightning Source LLC
Chambersburg PA
CBHW072300170526
45158CB00003BA/1130